ARE YOU READY TO BECOME YOUR OWN BOSS?

Strategies for Anyone, Anywhere, in Any Field

WORKBOOK

MELINDA F. EMERSON

www.BecomeYourOwnBossBook.com

Published by MFE Consulting, L.L.C.
P.O. Box 280 Drexel Hill, PA 19026
www.melindaemerson.com

ISBN: 978-0-9799839-1-7

Printed in the United States of America.
10 9 8 7 6 5 4 3 2 1

This publication is designed to provide accurate and authoritative information with regard to the subject matter covered. It is sold with the understanding that the publisher is not engaged in rendering legal, accounting, or other professional advice. If legal advice or other expert assistance is required, the services of a competent professional person should be sought.

This workbook, and the accompanying book Become Your Own Boss in 12 Months are available at quantity discounts for bulk purchases. For information, call 1-610-352-0680.

TABLE OF CONTENTS

ACKNOWLEDGMENTS

To all the entrepreneurs who dare to dream big.

I have an incredible kitchen cabinet of friends and mentors who helped me in all sorts of ways to finish this book and workbook project. They did research, read early drafts, gave pep talks, and helped me strategize about this book, and I love you all dearly. They include Gabrielle Ingram, Gina Stikes, Cassandra Hayes, Paul B. Brown, Renée Sloan, Laron Barber, Ramon Ray, Taris Mullins, Ray McKee, Rodney Emerson, Mark Corbin, Gerry Davis, Mary Meder, Paula Miller-Lester, Charles Dupree, Peter Archer, Cynthia McClain-Hill, Anisha Robinson, George Miles, Patty Walker, Darryl Ford-Williams, Anita Campbell, Janet Hill-Talbert, Evangelia Biddy, LiRon Anderson-Bell, Don Lafferty, Sharon G. Hadary, Gwen Martin, Cheryl Beth Kuckler, Sally Solis-Cohen, E. Steven Collins, Lisa Duhart Collins, Harold Strong, Will Gist, Maurice Goodman, Mel Gravely and Robin Bischoff.

I must thank my Quintessence family. You guys are my rock and my salvation. A heartfelt thanks to Joe Heastie, Jin Hong Kim, Morris Anderson, Michael Leftwich, Vince Wright, Lorna Neysmith, Eliu Cornielle, Julian Berrian, Troy Daniels, Bill Ladson, Herb Briley, Thomas Hooper, Luis Martinez, Vanessa Dawson, Indira Wilburn, Dianne Thompson, Frank Williams, Felix Beyard, Simone Williams, Robin Wideman, Latosha Ford Robinson, Tracey Johnson, Chris Conner, Jeanie Brister, Tesha Kelley and my former interns Felicia Commodore and Brittany Cunningham.

To my MFE Consulting, LLC dream team, You guys rock: Sonia Schenker, Cathy Larkin, Amy Larrimore, Kevin Lyons, Sweetie Berry, Scott Bradley, Eric Emerson, Marcia Perry, Tracey Reed and Loreen Brown.

I also must thank my Virginia Tech family. I summoned the courage to write this book and workbook because of a comment made to me by my former editorial writing professor, Dr. Kenneth Rystrom the day I graduated from college. He said, "You have a gift. One day you will be discovered for something that you write." I dismissed it at the time, but I am starting to believe he was on to something.

I am proud to be a member of the Hokie Nation. I must thank many of my fellow alumni and former professors. Dr. Calvin Jamison and Vera Turner were great resources, thanks so much to both of you. I must also thank Dr. Hayward Farrar, my eternal mentor and friend, for being such a great encourager. Dean LayNam Chang and his staff Debbie Wilson, Diane Stearns, Carolyn Furrow were also a big help to me. I thank you all so much for believing in this project.

Extra thanks to the team at NACCE including Executive Director Heather Van Sickle and my pal Matthew Montoya and Staci Scott at Community College of Philadelphia and Michael J. Critelli.

PROGRAM DESIGN TEAM

Melinda F. Emerson, Morris Anderson, MBA, Tai Goodwin, Instructional Designer, Gerda Gallop-Goodman, Kindra Cotton, Sabryna Washington, Graphic Design www.ingenuity7.com

WELCOME MESSAGE

I am grateful to have the opportunity to be an entrepreneur. I developed this curriculum to help others also know the joy of following their dreams to become their own boss. I believe the only way to build wealth in America is through small business ownership. I love entrepreneurs. I think they are the bravest people in the world. Everyone has good ideas. It is not lack of understanding how to start and run a small business that gets people in trouble. The *Are You Ready to Become Your Own Boss?* course and workbook are designed to give would-be entrepreneurs the tools needed make the decision whether or not to start their small business. After taking this course, students will be ready to move forward (or not) and complete the planning phase of their new enterprise and then launch a profitable and sustainable small business.

The failure rate for small businesses is high. According to a study by the U.S. Small Business Association only two-thirds of all small business startups survive the first two years, and less than half make it to four years. I think this happens for five basic reasons. First, people need a life plan before they ever write a business plan. Why? Small business owners must have a clear understanding what their life will be like as an entrepreneur. Next, many small business owners do not build up their network of contacts prior to starting a business. This is important because it is often where a new business will get its first customers. Third, entrepreneurs typically do not save enough money prior to starting a business, and then they do not have enough "runway" to give their business a chance to take off. Another big mistake small business owners often make is not having a target customer. They will try to sell to everyone, not just the customers interested in their product or service. Finally, too many entrepreneurs don't understand the need for fiscal discipline. Most successful businesses have solid financial controls in managing revenues and expenses.

My nickname is SmallBizLady and my mission is to improve your chances for entrepreneurial success. I wrote the book *Become Your Own Boss in 12 Months* and developed this course and workbook to reduce the learning curve of would-be entrepreneurs everywhere.

After participating in this course, you will know definitively whether you have a viable business idea and if you are personally prepared to become an entrepreneur. The Are You Ready to Become Your Own Boss? course and workbook are part of a wide range of resources I provide to help entrepreneurs. I have created a blog www. SucceedAsYourOwnBoss.com, which provides tools and tips for emerging entrepreneurs, and #Smallbizchat is a weekly live chat on Twitter that features top business experts.

For more information on the national bestseller, *Become your Own Boss in 12 Months* or the business training program, Are Your Ready to Become Your Own Boss? go to www.becomeyourownbossbook.com or call 610-352-0680.

To Your Business Success,

Melinda F. Emerson

PURPOSE

Welcome to *Are You Ready to Become Your Own Boss?* Most people dream about owning and running a business. You may have had a "notion" for years that someday you would be CEO of your own company; successful beyond your wildest dreams. Turning that dream into reality is an evolutionary process, involving not only having a solid business idea, but also understanding what you really want out of life. Then you need to make sure that you understand the "business of running a business." You are one idea away from being able to do anything you have ever wanted.

The purpose of this workbook is to walk you through Phase I of a three-step process to starting your small business. This workbook is a companion to the book, *Become Your Own Boss in 12 Months*, which is broken down into three parts: Get Ready, Get Set and Go. This workbook focuses on the "Get Ready" section of the book, which will help you lay out your personal long-term goals, get clarity on your personal and business financial picture, understand your personal strengths and weaknesses, clarify your specific business concept and develop a marketing plan. Once you complete this workbook, you will know definitively whether or not you should move forward with your business concept. Think of this workbook as your go/no go decision guide. To achieve success as a small business owner, you need to be flexible, pay close attention to your market and figure out what you do not know about running a business. The important thing is to start your business with a plan for yourself and your new enterprise.

HOW TO USE THIS WORKBOOK

- Set aside time
- Don't do it all in one sitting
- Read the book *Become Your Own Boss in 12 Months*
- Do the exercises
- Join the online community www.SucceedAsYourOwnBoss.com

Throughout the workbook you will see icons that reflect the following:

 Action Step

 Reflection

 Reality Check

THE EMERSON PLANNING SYSTEM

The key to being a successful entrepreneur is not only creating a sound business concept, but also taking the time to recognize what you don't know about operating that business.

The questions in this workbook guide you through using the Emerson Planning System to help you create one of your most important documents, your marketing plan. Many of the questions will be expanded in detail in later chapters for inclusion in your marketing plan. If you are able to produce a solid marketing plan, this provides validation that there is a market for your product or service. Then it will be time to move over to Phase II, which is developing a complete business plan.

This is a great time to explore entrepreneurship; you just need to make sure that the business you start is the right business for you. This planning process may seem like an exercise, but it's really an opportunity to think everything through. You will be able to personally plan, grow, and research your business idea to make sure you are ready to meet the task of starting your small business.

There are no right or wrong answers. The explanations provided along with each question are meant to clarify why your answer is important and to get you thinking about issues you may not have considered.

When you start a business, your time and money are on the line, and so are your dreams. Don't put your dreams at risk by not doing enough research and thoughtful planning.

There are six stages in the Emerson Planning System, which are broken out into three phase, Phase 1: Get Ready, Phase 2: Get Set and Phase 3: Go. This workbook is focusing on Phase 1.

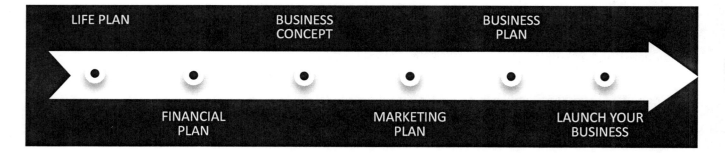

PHASE 1: THE "GET READY" PLANNING PHASE BEGINS HERE

Step I: LIFE PLAN is about getting clear about what you want out of life, so that you can build a business around your big picture vision for your life. You need to make sure that you are starting the right business for you and your family.

Step 2: FINANCIAL PLAN is about evaluating where you are financially. In this step, you will be able to determine whether or not you can afford to become an entrepreneur. You'll also have the ability to map out a plan to financially reposition yourself to eventually pursue your entrepreneurial dream.

Step 3: BUSINESS CONCEPT is about getting clarity around what you are selling and the business model you are pursuing. At the same time, you'll be looking at the skills that you have and need to run this particular type of business.

Step 4: MARKETING PLAN is about finding out whether there is a viable market for your business idea. If you can't define up front who's buying from you and why, you will have your answer about whether or not you should pursue this business idea.

PHASE II: THE "GET SET" PLANNING PHASE BEGINS HERE

Step 5: BUSINESS PLAN is about creating your roadmap for small business success. Once you have a marketing plan, you'll be able to flush out the rest of the business plan, including how you will handle operations, accounting, legal and human resources.

EMERSON'S ESSENTIALS

Just because you have a good idea and skills doesn't mean that you should run a business.

PHASE III: THE "GO" PLANNING PHASE BEGINS HERE

Step 6: QUIT THE JOB is about planning your exit from full-time employment. You should ideally start a business while you are still working. This step will allow you to develop support systems to manage your job and your business as long as you can.

EMERSON ESSENTIALS: Everybody's got good ideas and skills, but that does not mean they should become an entrepreneur. The business of running a business is an entirely different matter.

YOUR LIFE PLAN

After answering the questions in this section you will have:

- A clear picture of what you want your ideal life to look like
- Mapped out your motives for starting your business
- Assessed your values and work style to ensure that the entrepreneurial lifestyle is for you
- Reviewed your current lifestyle to identify the changes you will need to make to launch and run your business

Do you know what you want out of life as an entrepreneur? The dream of financial independence, being your own boss, satisfying a deeply held ambition, or creating your own enterprise are just a few of the things that people want from owning their own business. Articulate what your expectations are in being a business owner.

REALITY CHECK

Describe your ideal life? Where would you live? How much would you be working? How much free time do you want to have? What would your workday look like? Clarity here is important. Now describe what you imagine your life will look like for the first three years of running your business.	It's important to understand that as a new business owner, your ideal lifestyle may not become available to you immediately. Too many new entrepreneurs start strong only to give up once they realize the time, money, and energy it takes to get a business of the ground. Make sure you have a real clear understanding what your life could look like during the first three years.

It's important to understand that as a new business owner, your ideal lifestyle may not become available to you immediately. Too many new entrepreneurs start strong only to give up once they realize the time, money, and takes to get a business off the ground. Make sure you have a very clear understanding what your life could look like during the first three years.

WHAT ARE THE REALITIES OF YOUR LIFE TODAY?

Most of us do not live in a vacuum of interaction. We are immersed in the human experience of stress, family, work, health, wealth and concern about the future. Most of us can gauge our situations from "Couldn't be better" (10) to "It's a disaster" (1). Your reality today can directly impact the probability of your business success because of the possible emotional and financial distractions with which you have to deal.

On a scale of 1-10 (with 10 being excellent and 1 being disaster), rate the following areas of your life. For items that rank a 7 or below, write down 2 or more things you can do to improve that area.

AREA	RATING	ACTION ITEMS
Job		
Spouse / Relationship		
Kids		
Hobbies		
Self-care*		
Finances		
Friends/Social Life		
Spirituality		

*Self-care is all about how well you take care of yourself. (i.e. exercise, diet/nutrition, sleep, doctor visits, etc.)

WHAT'S YOUR MOTIVATION?

There may be a great market opportunity for your idea, you've been laid off from your job, you feel underused and under-appreciated in your position, or you are convinced that you can do a better job than the folks with whom you currently work.

WHY ARE YOU STARTING YOUR BUSINESS?

- Write down, in detail, why you want to be in business for yourself and what excites you about being an entrepreneur.

HOW WOULD YOU RANK YOUR MOTIVATION?

Understanding your motivation up front helps you figure out how best to set up your business. It boils down to five basic emotional drivers: Control, Freedom, Money, Problem Solving and Creativity. Your commitment to them will vary from extremely important to not important. Develop your profile and your level of motivation using the following chart.

Entrepreneurship Motivation Scale	Extremely Important	Somewhat Significant	Neutral	Somewhat Important	Not Important
Control					
Freedom					
Money					
Problem Solving					
Creativity					

Do you have confidence that your business will be successful? Your gut feelings may not be the best indicator of potential success. Getting as much factual information as you can is critical. Your key insight should be your competitive advantage. Knowing that you can give your customers something unique in the marketplace should reinforce your belief and confidence that your idea is viable. List the factors that give your business its edge.

Do you understand the energy and effort that will be required to make your business successful?
Hard work is a given for a successful business; a lazy attitude does not usually get you very far. More importantly, understanding the need for continuous learning about your market, your customer, finances, just so you can be a bit smarter today than you were yesterday, cannot be overstressed. Describe your work ethic and the things you've studied/learned in the last year to get ready for your business venture.

IS YOUR PERSONALITY SUITED TO THE BUSINESS?

There are certain personality traits commonly found in successful entrepreneurs. They include such factors as persistence, strong need to achieve, creativity, a high tolerance for risk, self-confidence, visionary, adaptive and a total commitment to success. Many successful entrepreneurs had a role model to influence them early on; some had parents who were entrepreneurs. Virtually all successful businesses start out as being personality driven. The consummate belief in your product or service and your need to tell others in person, through TV, radio, newspapers, flyers, web sites, e-mail, Twitter, blogs and other media is the driving force in getting out your message. Outgoing personalities are dominant (but not exclusive) in most entrepreneurs. Outline your strengths and what they will do for your business.

Which of the following traits typically found in successful entrepreneurs do you possess?

Trait	This Is Me	I'll Work On It	Don't Think I Need It
Persistence			
Strong need to achieve			
Creativity			
Willing to take risk			
Self-confidence			
Committed to success			
Adaptive			
Focused			
Visionary			

ACTIVITY: Ask three people who know you wlel what traits they see in you. This is helpful because sometimes others can see in us things we overlook. There are also times when we overestimate ourselves. Feedback from people we trust can give us a more complete picture.

WHERE ARE YOU IN YOUR PERSONAL LIFE?

Do you have family support? For example, do you have small children? Are you recently married or divorced? As an entrepreneur, your business life and personal life are like Siamese twins bound at the hip. It is challenging to manage given the mingling of finances, relationships, responsibilities, and priorities. If your family is not on board with your dream, there will indeed be some difficult decisions to be made. Try to gauge the level of support/ enthusiasm from your family and outline your strategy for sustaining and growing their help for your dream.

If you need more support, what are your options? Who else can you include on your team? (partner, mastermind group? Do you mean an advisory group?, virtual assistant, nanny or retired parent)

EMERSON ESSENTIALS: Take the time to plan your business. The best idea in the world doesn't make a great company; but a sound business plan does.

EMERSON'S ESSENT

Take the time
to plan
your business

WHAT ARE THE SKILLS THAT WOULD MAKE YOU SUCCESSFUL IN THIS BUSINESS?

An assessment of your current skill sets as they relate to your proposed business is critical. If you are making a natural transition into a business in which you are already experienced, you will have a shorter learning curve than if you are going into an area that is brand-new to you. To make your business work, you will have to already have the necessary skills, learn them or pay someone to do them. Make an inventory of your skills and the skills needed for your business.

List the top 10 skills you will need to use in your business. Then, determine what category that skill falls into. For skills that you need practice for, think about how you can get the experience or skills you need:

R= Ready   **N=Need Practice**   **L = Will Learn**   **O= Can Outsource**

	Skills Needed			Assessment
1				
2				
3				
4				
5				
6				
7				
8				
9				
10				

EMERSON ESSENTIALS: Everyone has tangible skills, but most people do not have all the skills needed to run a business. Moreover, small business owners typically underestimate what they need to get started in business.

EMERSON'S ESSENTIALS

Don't underestimate the skills you need to run a business

HOW DO YOU WANT TO WORK?

If you only want to work four days a week, then a goal of opening a retail store may not be for you. Use the following chart to identify how you like to work. This assessment will help you focus on doing what you love in the way most compatible to your style, so you can operate at your full potential.

HOW DO YOU WORK BEST	Extremely Important	Somewhat Important	Neutral	Somewhat Important	Not Important
Traditional 40 Hours					
Less than 40 hours					
Flexible work hours					
From a home office					
In an office setting with others					
Working independently					
Working with a team					
Interacting with lots of people on a daily basis					
Ocassional travel					
Aggressive travel					

DO YOU HAVE ENOUGH TIME TO FOCUS ON MAKING YOUR BUSINESS A SUCCESS?

Setting a timeframe and/or circumstances to remain in business or not will depend on how much money you have to keep things going and your sales/profitability trend. Not surprisingly, non-business factors – health, family relationships, stress and declining enthusiasm – are also important success determinants. Think about how much time you will allow to be successful, and, if you fail, what will be your exit strategy.

EMERSON ESSENTIALS: It is important to know how you work best. Can you handle working from home? Set boundaries with your family and friends and develop systems to separate work life and home life.

EMERSON'S ESSENTIALS

Knowing how you work best is vital to your success.

Map out the number of hours you currently spend on each item.

	Monday	Tuesday	Wednesday	Thursday	Friday	Saturday	Sunday
Work							
Commute time							
Child/Dependent Care							
Excercise							
Sleep							
Volunteer Activities							
Television/Internet							
Social Activities							
Other							

Now revise your allocation to reflect where you will make time to invest in your business.

	Monday	Tuesday	Wednesday	Thursday	Friday	Saturday	Sunday
Work							
Commute time							
Child/Dependent Care							
Excercise							
Sleep							
Volunteer Activities							
Television/Internet							
Social Activities							
Other							

HOW WILL YOU CHANGE YOUR LIFESTYLE TO SUPPORT YOUR TRANSITION INTO BEING AN ENTREPRENEUR?

Unless you are already rich, you will typically have to make some sacrifices in your current lifestyle which could include: taking fewer or no vacations, keeping your car a few more years, having very limited discretionary income, having a tight budget, and even caring what your friends think about your reduced lifestyle (I don't understand the last item). Make a list of those things that you are prepared to give up for your new business venture.

DECLARE YOUR COMMITMENT

When I started writing this book, I had no shortage of time commitments as a wife, mother and business owner. I made a contract with myself to get up at 5 a.m. and write two hours a day before my family started their day. With that discipline, I accomplished my goal of finishing my book and getting it to my editor on time.

Write Your Self-Contract

> Here's what I am going to do to start my business....

PERSONAL DEVELOPMENT PLAN

Which of the following items will you commit to in order to build your skills and expertise?

- Join an organization so you can network with others
- Join an industry association
- Read blogs (such as my blog http://www.SucceeAsYourOwnBoss.com)
- Register for a class
- Read books and magazines

EMERSON ESSENTIALS: Use Google to stay on top of your business and potential client base.

Set up a Google reader account for yourself which will function like your own newspaper. You must have a Gmail account to use any extra Google functions other than Google search.

EMERSON'S ESSENTIALS
Use Google to stay on top of your business and potential client base.

YOUR FINANCIAL PLAN

As you prepare to take the leap into entrepreneurship, you must consider your financial situation. It could be a real test if you have to cut back to the bare necessities. Are you willing to reduce your lifestyle down to just basic living expenses? It will take time to scale-down and to cut back to basics. The change in lifestyle will affect you and your family. And, depending on their ages, your children (teenagers especially) could really feel the pinch. Without sufficient preparation, including convening family meetings, creating a debt management strategy and having money available for dire emergencies, the stress in getting your business off the ground will be even more overwhelming.

This set of workbook questions takes you down to the next level of detail in getting you prepared financially to open your business in 12 months. The objective is to minimize as much downside risk as possible — preparation is the best way to avoid failure and reduce the impact of potential obstacles.

HOW IS YOUR OVERALL FINANCIAL CONDITION?
On a scale of 0-5, with 0 being a disaster, and 5 being solid, rate your current financial condition.

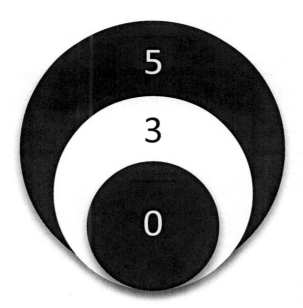

CAN YOU AFFORD TO BECOME AN ENTREPRENEUR?
This will depend on whether or not you will be a full-time entrepreneur or a start a side hustle business. How will you pay the rent/mortgage, utility bills, food, college tuition, clothing and other life expenses, that generally don't go away if you decide to go into business for yourself? Having a financial plan to meet these obligations is essential. Making a profit in your enterprise before you run out of capital to sustain should be your key goal(Please clarify—this sentence doesn't make sense to me.). Provide a general idea of how you are going to do this.

CHECKLIST

Do you have the following?

- Zero debt
- 6 months of emergency savings
- Credit score of 700 or higher
- 12 month household budget
- 1st year of operating expenses

Can you answer yes to each one of these? This is ideally where you need to be before you start your business full-time.

ARE YOU FINANCIALLY PREPARED FOR YOUR FIRST YEAR OF BUSINESS?

A high FICA score, low debt and solid personal credit are keys to a successful business launch, especially if there is significant capital needed for start-up. If you are going into business full-time, a year's worth of savings to pay household expenses, enough money to get your business to break-even, and 4-5 months of emergency cash are ideal. Anything less than these benchmarks could make your business launch difficult. List your liquid assets (cash, bonds, etc.) and compare to your current debt (See question #3 above)

Current Liabilities	Can I Support Myself for 1 Year?	If Not, How Much Money Do I Need?
Fixed Expenses		
Variable Expenses		
New Business Start-up Costs		
Annual Business Operating Costs		

WHAT IS YOUR PLAN TO REDUCE/ELIMINATE DEBT?

Developing a strategy to reduce your debt is first on the list of things you need to consider. Consider securing a home equity loan (which can have positive tax benefits), tapping your 401K (which can have negative tax implications), refinancing your mortgage, using savings, selling stocks or other assets to pay down credit card debt, student loans, or other short-term debt. These are solid approaches to getting your personal credit in order. List the things you want to do today to improve your credit and what you plan to do over the next few months.

WHAT DOES YOUR CREDIT REPORT REVEAL?

Having a good credit score (700 or higher) is important when starting out in business. You will need vendors and others to extend you credit. The only tool they will have to consider is your personal credit score. Your personal credit is your business' credit. When you look at a retail space, and want to sign a lease, the landlord will pull your credit score. If you need a merchant service account to accept credit cards, the vendor will pull your credit score. If you ever plan to borrow money or apply for a line of credit, your personal credit score is the most important information in the application process.

Get your credit report. TransUnion®, Equifax®, and Experian® Credit will each provide a free credit report once a year, but you must pay for your actual credit score. Get all three scores, as each credit bureau scores differently. You can also use www.annualcreditreport.com to get a free credit report. List your current credit scores and address any negative information that may be on them.

Is your credit report in good shape? If not, what will you do to get it in good shape?

WHAT'S YOUR NET WORTH?

It's important to know your net worth, that is, the value of everything you own subtracted from everything you owe. It is the clearest indicator of your wealth. If you owe more than you own, it could impact you becoming a business owner. Complete the following chart to see where you stand.

EMERSON ESSENTIALS: Nobody will buy into your dream if you don't. Your personal cash reserves must be invested in your business, but please consider all the risks before spending your life savings on your business idea.

EMERSON'S ESSENTIALS

Nobody will buy your dreams if you don't

YOUR NET WORTH WORKSHEET

Current Liabilities	Can I Support Myself for 1 Year?	If Not, How Much Money Do I Need?
Fixed Expenses		
Variable Expenses		
New Business Start-up Costs		
Annual Business Operating Costs		

ASSETS	AMOUNT
List the balances in your accounts and the market value of your assets	
Bank accounts (savings, checking)	
401(k)s, mutual funds, other retirement accounts	
Insurance cash value	
Vehicles	
Real Estate	
Personal property (furniture, antiques, jewelry, etc.)	
Other asset (What about stocks and bonds?)	
Other asset	
Other asset	
Other asset	
TOTAL ASSETS	

LIABILITIES	AMOUNT
List the unpaid balances of the following types of loans, along with any other debt. Enter numbers in the cells next to the type of liability.	
Mortgage	
Vehicle loan	
Other debt (What about student loans and credit cards?	
Other debt	
Other debt	
TOTAL LIABILITIES	
NET WORTH = TOTAL ASSETS - TOTAL LIABILITIES (A-B)	

WHAT ARE THE BENEFITS YOU ARE GOING TO MISS THE MOST WHEN YOU QUIT YOUR JOB?

Health and life insurance, 401Ks, paid vacation days, business travel opportunities, and a 40-hour workweek come to mind as some of the benefits of corporate life. Being prepared to compensate for these lost perks (if you currently have them) when you are self-employed could be a challenge. List the items you will miss the most and describe how you plan to replace/offset them.

Benefit	Current	Planned Offset
Health/Life Insurance		
Pension Plan		
Vacation		
Sick Days		
401K		
Stock Options		
40-hour workweek		

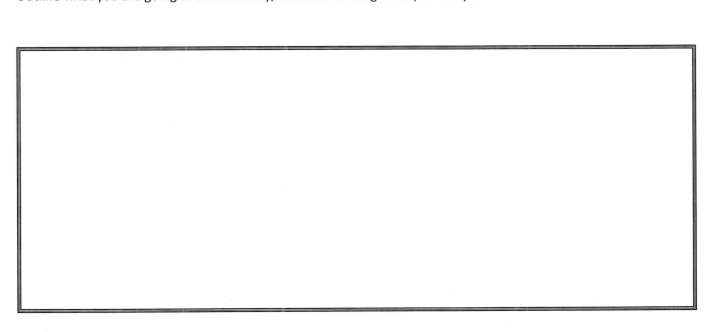

WHAT ARE YOUR PLANS FOR HEALTH AND LIFE INSURANCE?

Predicting illness for ourselves or our family members is nearly impossible. It is estimated that 50% of all bankruptcies are caused by medical bills or illness. Even with insurance, high co-payments, deductibles, exclusions from coverage and loopholes left many holding the bag for thousands of dollars in medical expenses. Outline what you are going to do for family/business coverage and provide your estimated cost.

DO YOU HAVE A HOUSEHOLD BUDGET?

Fill it out with your current revenues/expenses and then, reviewing each category, project what your goals are and in what time period they will be achieved.

Income	Monthly Amount	Anuualized	Percent
Net Pay			
Second Job - Net Pay			
Investments			
Interest			
Other			
Total Income	$	$	100%

Routine (or Fixed) Expenses	Monthly Amount	Anuualized	Percent
Cable TV			
Car Payments			
Child Care			
Credit Card Payments			
Insurance (health, life and property			
Internet Service Provider			
Rent or Mortgage			
Student Loans			
Taxes			
Telephone			
Utilities			
Other			
Total Routine Expenses	$	$	100%

Variable Expenses	Monthly Amount	Anuualized	Percent
Babysitting			
Food			
Transportation (incl. gas maintenance, parking, and taxis)			
Vacation			
Clothing (Purchases, Dry Cleaning)			
Education			
Entertainment			
Gifts (Birthdays, Holidays, Weddings)			
Haircare, bodycare (hair cuts, manicures, tanning)			
Medication, Doctor Visits, Glasses/ Contacts			
Savings			
Other			
Total Variable Expenses	$	$	100%

Total Monthly Fixed and Variable Expenses	$
Difference between Monthly Income and Expenses: surplus/(deficit)	$

By taking the time now to run your household with a budget, you will be far more likely to run your business with one, which will be a key skill to have as you start your business.

EMERSON ESSENTIALS: Lack of personal and fiscal discipline is one of the top reasons why small businesses fail. You must make business decisions based on up-to-date financial information. Utilize an accountant to keep your financial records up to date and use a budget to run your business. Be sure to ask yourself why three times before making any purchases for your business.

EMERSON'S ESSENTIALS

Lack of personal and fiscal discipline is one of the top reasons why small businesses fail

START THINKING LIKE AN ENTREPRENEUR

I once heard a man say, "You are one idea away from accomplishing anything you want." This is a true statement. Entrepreneurs are visionaries. They see the big picture. They are leaders and innovators. Most believe they can build a better mousetrap. Sometimes visionaries have too broad and grandiose visions, though. They want a billion dollar IPO like Google; a million dollar business is not enough.

Confidence in your ability and your product or service is essential, but the business vision must be realistic. You cannot project $2 million in revenue in the first year with a staff of two people. You need to define the business vision by your core services or products, your unique value proposition, the year-to-year revenue growth, and ultimately, how big you want the company to become long-term. Your business vision is the articulation of what you see your business becoming. Ideally, it becomes a self-fulfilling prophecy. You want your prophecy built on solid information.

The next set of questions is designed to help you align your business dreams with reality and to make sure your expectations are set at the right level.

Successful Entrepreneurs	Do You?	Why Should You...
Get outside advice for their business.		Successful business owners understand the value of having a skilled network of professionals to help with areas outside of their expertise. Sometimes a phone call to an advisor can save a lot of heartburn and money.
Have an entrepreneurial mindset.		To win at being an entrepreneur requires that you shift from thinking like a worker bee to thinking more strategically about how you will create the opportunities and resources needed to grow your business.
Set healthy boundaries that help family and friends understand that their "time is money."		It is important to create an informal set of rules for yourself outlining when and how you want to communicate with friends and family.
Know how to stay motivated.		There will be times when you will be doing your best, but feel frustrated by a lack of progress in your business. Staying motivated, minimizing your frustration and avoiding negative thinking are key elements to keeping your business on track.
Develop critical milestones based on the specific goals.		Creating some general goals for what you would do before an event happens provides some definite planning advantages. Outline your critical milestones and speculate on your response if they succeed or if they fail.

TIPS:

- Keep the company of smart people.
- You will need to develop relationships with people who are already entrepreneurs or other business people in a position to give great insight into what you need to do because they have been there and done that.
- To develop a mindset for success, you must realize that how you perceive your business and your life can define your reality.
- Entrepreneurs are willing to fail to eventually win. They understand that not every idea is a good one. Real entrepreneurs learn from failure and move on to the next big idea.

THINK LIKE AN ENTREPRENEUR: ACTION PLAN

1. Advisors That Can Help Build My Business

Role	How can they help?	Who do I know?
Accountant		
Legal Advice		
Web Design		
Graphic Design		
Marketing/Advertising		
PR		
Human resources		
Sales		

NEXT STEP: HOW WILL YOU REACH OUT TO THESE PEOPLE ON A CONSISTENT BASIS?

2. To think like an entrepreneur, start by reading what entrepreneurs read. Commit to spending 30 minutes each day reading from the following list:
    a. Smallbiztrends.com
    b. Smart Briefs on Business/Small Biz/etc.
    c. Entrepreneur magazine
    d. Fast Company magazine

3. Draft a letter you will send to friends and family that clearly communicates how they can support the boundaries you need to establish to run your business.

4. Imagine that it's five years from now and you have accomplished all of your business and life objectives. Write a letter from your future self to you today. What encouragement and words of wisdom would the future you provide? Whenever you are going through a rough patch, go back and read the wise words and words of encouragement.

5. Review your one-year, three-year, and five-year plans for your business. Are the milestones you identified measurable enough for you to gauge how well you are doing? Are they based on sales, profits, number of customers, or personal gains, like reduced stress or improved health?

YOUR BUSINESS BLUEPRINT

Now it's time to get into the work of creating a clear vision for your business. To do this, you'll be answering questions in three areas:

- What's Your Business?
- What's Your Marketing Plan?
- What's Your Plan for Getting Your Product/Service to Market?

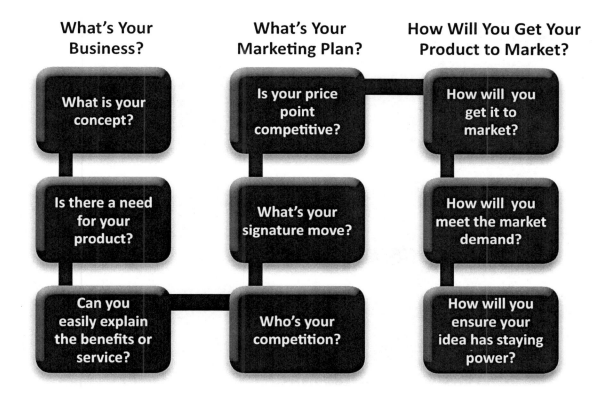

What's Your Business?
- What is your concept?
- Is there a need for your product?
- Can you easily explain the benefits or service?

What's Your Marketing Plan?
- Is your price point competitive?
- What's your signature move?
- Who's your competition?

How Will You Get Your Product to Market?
- How will you get it to market?
- How will you meet the market demand?
- How will you ensure your idea has staying power?

EMERSON ESSENTIALS: When you start a niche business you can spend more time generating business and less time looking for the market. You can focus on generating a message and value proposition that appeals to them.

EMERSON'S ESSENTIALS

Having a Budget is essential for any small business.

WHAT'S YOUR BUSINESS?

YOUR BUSINESS CONCEPT

Refining your business concept is the next phase of your journey as an entrepreneur. You must spend a significant amount of time determining if your business idea is viable. The work you do today will save you both time and money and give you insight into many of the roadblocks you'll face. Here are the main questions that will help you define the best model for your business.

In 100 words or less, describe your business concept.

NAMING YOUR PRODUCT OR SERVICE

Naming your business can be difficult. You want it to be catchy and memorable, but you also want to make sure you are taken seriously. Most importantly, you want a name that will work now—and in the future. Using your last name in naming your business is always a safe bet. Using the last name of the business owner by itself or along with words that describe the business activity is a perfect legal name. By using your last name, you do not need to file a fictitious name form with your state to go into business. Anderson Consulting, LLC is a perfect example of this. Partnerships work the same way. The last name of all partners can stand alone, or be used with words that describe the business.

TIPS FOR NAMING YOUR BUSINESS

1. **Avoid use of a word that is hard to say or spell.** It simply annoys people, and it will be harder for Internet searches to find your firm, unless you purchase all of the URLs for the misspelled versions of your business name as well. My first company was Quintessence Multimedia—trust what I am saying.

2. **Do not create a new word.** It's never a good idea to have people scratching their head wondering what a word means.

3. **Do not use words that are so common that they are easily forgettable.** Always display your uniqueness and make your business memorable.

4. **Avoid purposefully misspelled words.** Do not add numbers, odd letters, or dashes in your business name to make it work on the Internet. Spell cat with a 'c' not a 'k'. Do not use words that share letters. If your business has two 'c''s back to back, do not confuse people by using one 'c' just because that domain name is available. Boyz & Girlz clothes, Ruthtele-communications.com, and ML4T are examples of what not to do.

5. **Do an Internet search to check your business name.** As you are deciding on a name for your business, always do an Internet search to see if the URL is available. If you do not (Do you mean if you do find someone?)find someone using your name, you have two choices: find another name or create the URL with inc, online, or llc after it or create a URL that just describes what you sell (i.e. bestpracticefundraising.com).

6. **Do not use the name of your town.** Think about where your clients will come from in 5 to 10 years. PNC Bank was once Pittsburgh National Bank. A name tied to your town can stifle your growth once you look outside your region for customers.

7. **Once you get in business, if you realize that your name no longer works—change it.** My first business was originally named Quintessence Entertainment, Inc. I finally changed it after the 100th call asking if we worked with or booked music acts. A name change is a great PR hook and an excuse to hold a grand re-opening.

8. **If you operate a business under a fictitious name,** you must register in the state where you plan to do business. The purpose for this registration is to create a public record of who owns the business to protect the public from fraud. Registering your fictitious name does not provide the business with exclusive rights to use the name. The same fictitious name can be used by different businesses.

When you incorporate your business, you earn the exclusive use of your corporate name in your state. Your corporate name may not be the same as, or confusingly similar to, the name of any other business. Depending on the state where you operate, there are penalties for failing to register a fictitious name. In Pennsylvania, where my business is located, unregistered businesses may not use the courts to enforce a contract using the fictitious name. The court also has the option of imposing a $500 penalty.

Make a list of the business names you want to consider. Research them and decide which one you want to protect.

Potential Name	Registered?	URL Available?

NICHE TO GET RICH

"Niche to get rich" certainly has a nice ring to it. Who doesn't want to get rich? What the heck is a niche? Webster's Business Dictionary defines a niche as "a particular market or specialty area where a company finds it profitable to concentrate its efforts". Niche marketing offers a concentration of clients in an area of limited competition. The key words here are "concentration of clients" and "limited competition"— sweet words for the budding entrepreneur. There is also a "market niche." A "market niche" can be a specific geographic area such the Mid-Atlantic region, a specialty industry such as sugar-free desserts, ethnic or age groups such a Generation Xers, or any other particular group of people, such as people who don't own cars (Since so many people own cars, what about using people who own poodles instead?). Niche businesses can also position themselves as specialists, charge more and generate higher profit margins. Profit margin is the net profit to the business after all expenses are paid to produce and deliver a product or service.

A niche can be anywhere from under (or on) your nose (think Breathe Right® strips for snorers), to cyberspace, where eBay® and YouTube®, among others, have generated millions. You might stumble on it. I spoke to a CPA friend of mine who only specializes in restaurant accounting. Do something that no one else will, like picking up dog poop (and make $50,000 per year like the folks at www.Poopbutler.com. Sometimes, a niche can be created by improving a common product already on the market. Think the Swiffer®, the sleek hand duster, or Splenda®, the sugar substitute. A business that focuses on addressing an unmet need can be a niche business too. Think grocery store chains in inner-cities, or a car sharing business for people with an occasional need for wheels.

HERE ARE SOME IDEAS FOR FINDING YOUR NICHE:

Go With What You Know	Bob spent many years in the tow truck business. He was located close to a major turnpike and the work was very competitive. He needed an edge to grow his business and decided to buy a tow truck that could tow and lift big rigs. There were no competitors within 50 miles, and his revenues rose 50% the first year because he was the only game in the area. He was an expert in towing and used his skills to specialize. Some popular niches include virtual call centers, personal training, beauty salons/spas, travel agencies, gyms, computer repair, technical/online support and business coaching. List the area(s) where you have some expertise.
Fill a gap that your current employer is not fulfilling.	If you work for a business like the one you plan to start, you may see a niche that your employer is ignoring. You can also learn what you should and should not do in your business. You will be far smarter about suppliers, customer requirements, costs, and pitfalls related to your potential business. You may also gain access to other markets that you never considered. A friend of mine worked for a major conglomerate early on in his career as a product manager. He saw an opportunity for the business where he was working to expand their services into a product area that would generate an additional $25 million in revenues a year. He researched the market and developed the business plan and presented the business case to his superiors. In the end, the company passed on the opportunity claiming that $25 million in revenues was not significant enough to dedicate the resources to pursue the opportunity. My friend realized that if they didn't want to pursue it, he could. So he worked for that business unit another nine months and then quit to start his firm. He has not quite hit $25 million yet, but he is closing in on it. Is there an opportunity you see that others don't? What is it?

Look for "You Must Be Kidding" Opportunities	The enterprising entrepreneur will find a pot of gold in everything from bathroom maintenance services, pest control, window washing, maintaining septic systems, to building a business pet sitting. Beauty is in the eye of the beholder and what some would see as unattractive jobs, others see as a key to the mint. Typically, if you pursue an "ugly" business, you can generally bet that the competitors will be few and the potential unlimited. Can you think of an "ugly" business that satisfies an unmet need? What is it?
Turn a Hobby into a Money Machine	Stories abound about cookie makers (Famous Amos, Mrs. Fields, etc.) who went from the kitchen to national enterprises because they were tuned into America's tastebuds. For example, a local toy store in my area grew out of the owner's affection for model trains. He now specializes in selling unique toy trains nationwide using the Internet. Do you think your hobby can be a money-making opportunity?
Invent Something	Mother Necessity is always looking for solutions to problems. The Butler Bag, PedEgg™, plastic garbage bags, the Jet Ski, and WD-40 are just a few of the many products created by inventors who made a niche where none existed before. Another great example, my friend Julia Rhodes created a product called KleenSlate Concepts™. As a teacher, she realized that children needed more flexible writing environments. She invented hand-held dry erase boards for children and schools. She also created a line of dry erase markers with the felt eraser tip attached to the marker. She also promoted her product in a unique way. She made clothes for herself out of her product and walked around trade shows writing on herself and then erasing it. Her stunts got her noticed by retailers and even got her a spot on the inventors showcase on The Tonight Show with Jay Leno. Her products are now sold through major office supply stores, national supply catalogs, and retail school supply chains nationwide. What's your idea?

FIND YOUR NICHE!

For each of the strategies on the next page, spend 5-7 minutes brainstorming potential niches. Two heads (or more) are better than one. Get a few associates from your network together and ask them to help you brainstorm.

Go With What You Know	
Fill a gap that your current employer is not fulfilling.	
Look for "You Must Be Kidding" Opportunities	
Turn a Hobby into a Money Machine	
Invent Something	

The quality of life that we know today was in no small part built on the creation of products and services that were either brand new or built on existing technology. If you can create an improvement that the public can embrace, congratulations, you are now a niche business owner!

DEFINING YOUR CUSTOMER PROFILE

Who needs your product or service?

Finding an unmet need in the marketplace can be a great business strategy. Many new ideas and products are built on existing concepts that fill an underserved niche. For example, the post office has always delivered packages, but Federal Express and UPS took that concept to the next level. It is all about solving customer problems or fulfilling customer wants or needs. Your marketing strategy should always be focused on addressing basic customer needs at the right price. A customer will not spend $5.00 to solve a 50 cent problem. They will spend $5.00 to solve a $50.00 problem. If you know the cost of the problem, you can provide real value in the price of your solution. If applicable, describe the business/customer problem that you are solving and the cost of your solution compared to your competitors.

Define your ideal client and why they need you.

The more focused you are on who your customer is, where they shop, where they live, how often they buy things, what their values are and what their struggles are, the easier it is to sell to them. For example, imagine you offer a product for working mothers with children under age 5. You could advertise on easy listening radio stations that women typically play at work. You could also advertise in Parenting, Cookie or Working Mother magazine. You reduce the risk of wasting money, by carefully qualifying your customer. By knowing your customer and their pain points (Explain what a pain point is), you can eliminate a lot of guess work and your marketing dollars will go a lot further. If you want to catch a fish, you have to go where hungry fish are swimming. Do you know who and where your potential customers are? Make a profile of your customer. The table on the next page can serve as a starting point.

Characteristic	Important	Non-Important	Why?
Age 18 to 30			
Age 31 to 45			
Income			
Ethnicity			
Home Ownership			
Gender			
Pet Owner			

This is just a sample approach to further define what your customer "looks" like and the common attributes they have that could impact a purchase decision.

Is it a money maker?

Last, but not least, how much money is in your market niche? What is the buying power of your niche market? How much do they spend in your industry? How much of the market share do you need to have to get beyond break even?

EMERSON'S TIPS

- The nature of business has changed. The best thing you can do for your business venture is to know your customers intimately. Niche marketing allows you to spend your marketing/advertising dollars more efficiently.
- Niche marketing also enables you to create momentum faster.
- Be known for something. The more you know, the better your expertise, the more you can charge and the stronger your chances of success.
- Passion for your business has its place, but it may not pay the bills. If things aren't growing as fast as you like, what is your plan "B" to maintain yourself (and perhaps your family)? Bill collectors are a pesky breed and not always sympathetic to your dreams.

CREATING YOUR MARKETING PLAN: EYEING WHO'S BUYING

Now that you've decided on your niche, it's time to develop your marketing plan. By developing your marketing plan before creating your business plan, you are giving yourself an opportunity to assess whether there's really a market for your product or service. This upfront analysis is the most important thing you can do before going into business.

If you can validate your market opportunity, you will have the answer to whether or not you should start your business. If you can identify who is buying and why they are buying from you, a sound business plan is not far behind. Your marketing plan is the foundation upon which your business plan is built.

So much goes into a solid marketing plan, everything from knowing the product offerings and benefits, to the customers (such as knowing about specific customer profiles (Gen X, Gen Y, Gen D, Baby Boomers, etc.)), to pricing, to competitive analysis and sales. Why bother? It is much easier and cheaper to do your homework before you open your doors than to scramble after the business is open. A good marketing plan forces you to think about your business growth potential and by ripple effect, the amount of profit you will generate. This is very important if you are trying to convince a bank or venture capitalist to loan you money.

MARKETING PLAN CHECK LIST

These are the critical questions your marketing plan should answer about your product or service.

- Can you explain your product or service with a signature message?
- Have you analyzed the total market opportunity for your product or service?
- Can you describe how your product or service will benefit your target market?
- Have you determined your positioning in the marketplace?
- Do you have a pricing strategy?
- Have you developed a signature move to stand out in the marketplace?
- What is the sales process for your new venture?
- What marketing and social media mix will you use to reach your target market?
- If your product features intellectual property, have you protected it?
- Do you have a sales forecast and marketing budget?
- How will you distribute your product?

Can you easily explain your product or service?

Sometimes you can put your business behind the eight ball by offering a product or service that requires too much explanation or is so new or unusual that you confuse people. More importantly, you do not want anyone confused about why they should buy it. You may spend the first year or two in business educating people about your product (understanding and using new cell phone features are a prime example). Mobilizing marketing campaigns to make the market aware of your product is not impossible, but very costly. Heavy advertising, out-of-the-box public relations approaches and social media strategies are necessary. Describe how you plan to educate the buying public about your product or service.

Outline the feature and benefits of your product or service.

Features	Benefits

Now that you've outlined the features and benefits of what you offer, can you summarize it succinctly in 50 words or less? How about 30 words or less? If you can get this down to six words or less, you might just have a great tagline! Messaging is key when trying to stand out in the marketplace whether it's online or in a face-to-face encounter. In any networking situation, you only have seven seconds to make an impression on a potential contact. A snappy tagline will help you hold the interest of a prospect.

In 50 Words or Less	In 30 Words or Less

Tying it all together

Now that you have done your due diligence in researching the market for your business, write three paragraphs, backed up with data, to show that your proposed business concept is a good idea.

This is a good business idea because...

In Case You Need More Space

Do your homework if you are offering a groundbreaking product. If there are few competitors, it will mean that you are ahead of the pack or there may not be enough customers to sustain your business. This is another opportunity for some sort of market research. Describe and list your potential competitors.

Estimate of total number of competing businesses: Local _____ National _____

Name	National or Local	Size	What They Offer or Do?	No. of Years in Business

Is your price point competitive?

When considering pricing, first survey the competition. Your price must cover your costs, emphasize the value you are providing the customer, and earn you a reasonable profit. Test your pricing strategy before going with it. The marketplace will quickly tell you if your price tag is too high. The wrong price tag is like a bad first impression. Most of the time, you do not get a second chance to make a first impression. Your strategy could be to be the high price (high value) provider. A salesperson for the top competitor to my multimedia company once told me, their company philosophy was to be the most expensive option in the market. It's a bold move, but if you spin it right, there are customers who will go for it if they see real value in your offering. Ultimately, pricing must be driven by the needs of the business. If you don't make a profit, what is the point in having a business in the first place? Check the price points being offered for your service or product, review your anticipated costs and determine if you can compete on price.

Competitor Name	Price	Estimated Cost	Margin	Your Price	Margin

How will you differentiate — what's your signature move?

Do you have a clear idea of your competitive advantage? What is your unique value proposition? How are you more special than the competition? You must have distinct differences. Anyone can sell purses, tires or provide marketing consulting. Why should anyone buy from you? To own the market, your potential clients must find exceptional value from your product or service.

List the factors that make your product or service special. See the following examples:

Your Competitive Advantage	Communicating Your Value
Low Price	TV and Newspaper Ads
Exclusivity	Client List
Quality	Testimonials
One-Stop Shop	Web site and online presence

Your Turn:

Your Competitive Advantage	Communicating Your Value

Product, Placement, Promotion, and Price are the four corners of marketing.

Once you have qualified the viability and size of your opportunity, you now must figure out how to close the deal. You can build a better mousetrap, but if no one knows about it, who cares? If the trap is too expensive and the customer does not consider it a real value, it will sit on store shelves. Your challenge is to make sure you've answered the important questions on the marketability of your product or service. Let's look at what these four basic elements mean and that you are clear as to how they relate to your proposed business.

- **Product:** Extensively describes your product or service including branding, size, options, quality, warranties and packaging. It answers the questions: How will it meet client needs, what geographic area will be served, what are the features and benefits of that product or service, and its competitive edge.

- **Placement:** How will your product/service be manufactured or performed? How will it be delivered? What are the distribution channels? It describes the physical facilities needed, i.e. warehouse, garage, fulfillment house, office space, strategic alliance facility or other area to support service for delivery.

- **Promotion:** Developing your marketing mix of activities, outlining what advertising channels you'll use to get the word out, i.e. flyers, magazine, newspapers, direct mail, telemarketing, Internet, radio/TV. Public relations strategies may include holding high-profile public events. Your business must reach out to your personal networks and potential customers using direct mail and social media. All activities should provide information on the value and impact of your new business' products or services.

- **Price:** You must know what the market will pay. Pricing strategy is all about pricing your product or service for your different target markets. You will need to determine the list price, discounts, wholesale, allowances, markdowns, payment periods, and credit terms. Based on your sales strategy, you need to decide if your product will have premium or discount pricing.

Strategy / Target	Product	Placement	Promotion	Price
Hi-End Customers	High Quality Exclusive Leather Goods	High-End Retail Stores, Targeted Mail-Order	Fortune, Wall Street Journal, NY Times	Premium - Rarely on Sale
Mass Market High/Middle-End customers	Good Quality Sweaters	Department Stores	Local Radio, Newspapers, Circulars, TV	High-End Competitive w/ some discounts
Teenagers	Embossed T-Shirts Comfort Wear	Specialty Young Wear Shops (GAP, Aeropostle, American Eagle, others)	Local Radio Newspapers, Circulars, TV, Word- of-Mouth	Medium – Low End Pricing – Big Discounts

The matrix above is just an example of how you want to think about your product or service. It is most important that your product is surrounded by the right strategy to maximize customer exposure and opportunity for sales.

EMERSON ESSENTIALS: By developing your marketing plan before creating your business plan, you are giving yourself an opportunity to assess whether there's really a market for your product or service.

EMERSON'S ESSENTI...

You should create your Marketing Plan before your Business Plan

PUTTING IT ALL TOGETHER

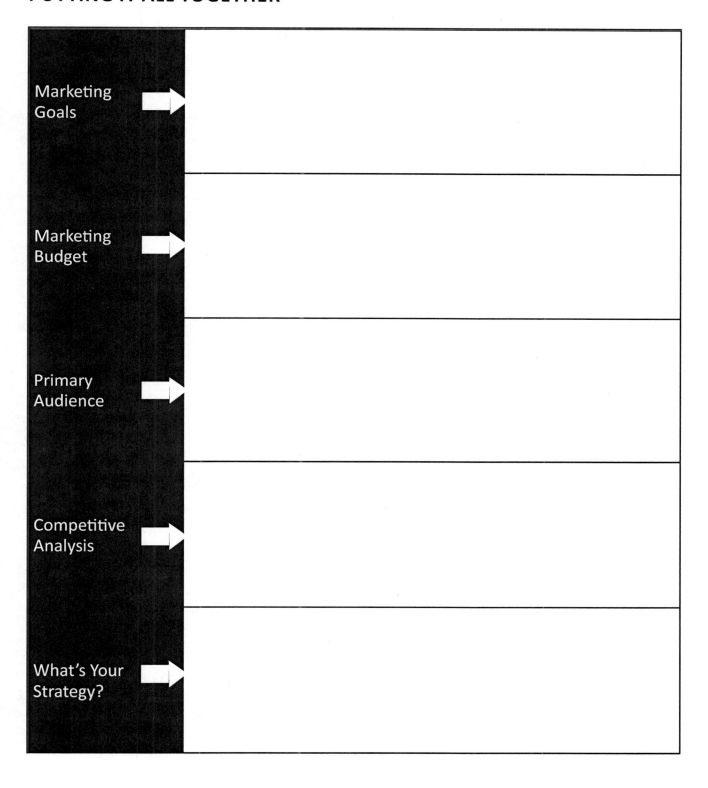

SAMPLE MARKETING PLAN

123 ACCOUNTING PLUS SOFTWARE (PRODUCT-BASED COMPANY)

NOTE: THIS MARKETING PLAN IS REPRINTED WITH PERMISSION FROM THE AUTHOR, KINDRA COTTON

Overall Goals of 123 Accounting Plus Software Marketing Strategy

The overall goals of 123 Accounting Plus Software Marketing Strategy are to: 1) establish a customer base for the product offered by the company, 2) keep current customers through product upgrades, and 3) increase product sales.

The primary goal of this marketing strategy is to identify and build a database of the best customers for our software product. Since 123 Accounting Plus Software is a relatively unknown name brand, the secondary goal of this marketing strategy is to implement a long-term branding strategy by keeping our current customers through software upgrades thus providing continued value to our customers. Establishing a loyal customer base and developing a recognized brand will lead to increased product sales, thereby realizing the final goal of the company's marketing strategy.

MARKET RESEARCH AND COMPETITIVE ANALYSIS

The National Small Business Environment

Often credited with creating innovative ideas and bringing new and dynamic products and services to the national economy, small businesses are the lifeblood of the American economy. Independent businesses with less than 500 employees, known as a "small business" Accountings for 99.7% of all employer firms in the U.S. and employ half of all private sector employees. There were an estimated 27.7 million small businesses in the U.S. in 2008, where 15.9 million (57%) were comprised of self-employed incorporated and unincorporated individuals, indicating a near 2% decrease from the previous year. Currently, the survival rate of new businesses is two years for approximately 2/3rds of all small businesses, with an estimated 44% surviving at least 4 years.

Small businesses have generated 60% to 80% of new net jobs annually, and created more than half of non-agricultural private gross domestic product (GDP) over the past 10 years, where home-based businesses make up slightly more than half (52%) of all small businesses and franchise ownership makes up approximately 2%.

The State of Tennessee Small Business Environment

In the State of Tennessee, there are an estimated total of 560,288 small businesses, where an estimated 16,770 new employer firms were created in 2008 amid one of the worse recessions seen in decades, resulting in a 13.6% decrease from the previous year. Also in 2008, business bankruptcies totaled 888, up from 537 in 2007, while business terminations increased to 18,373 in 2008 from 15,674 in 2007. Non-farm proprietors' income, which is a share of small business income, increased to $22.9 billion in 2008, up from $22.8 billion in 2007.

Trends within the State of Tennessee Small Business Environment

The following table shows the trends within the Small Business Environment in the State of Tennessee:

	Number of Estimated Small Businesses	New Employer Firms Created	Employer Firms Closed	Small Business Income (in billions $)
2004	471,316	17,415	16,520	$20.9
2005	513,000	17,484	17,135	$22.3
2006	531,200	17,207	16,400	$23.3
2007	536,750	19,401	15,674	$22.8
2008	560,288	16,770	18,373	$22.9
Average Yearly Increase/ Decrease	3.4% increase	0.5% decrease	3% increase	2.4% increase

On average the estimated number of small businesses in the State of Tennessee increases by 3.4% each year. While the number of new employer firms created appeared to show a 12.8% increase in the state in 2007, a 13.6% decline in 2008 brings the yearly average of new employer firms created to a decreasing 0.5% over the five year period from 2004 to 2008. The number of employer firms to close each year decreased about 1% annually until 2008 when there was a 17.2% increase in firm closures, yet despite the lower number of firms opening and increased number of closings, small business income from 2007 to 2008 showed an annual increase of approximately 2.4% during the five year period beginning in 2004.

Preliminary Market Research Conducted in Middle Tennessee

Primary market research was conducted by 123 Accounting Plus Software in order to get a better assessment of the target demographic of Small Business Owners in Middle Tennessee most likely to require the Accounting software made by the company. In 2007, there were approximately 38,676 small businesses (defined as businesses with less than 500 employees) in the Metropolitan Nashville-Davidson County-Murfreesboro, TN area. The following analysis focused on current business owners in the Middle Tennessee area, and asked them to provide feedback on their experiences with software programs, as well as identify some of their current software needs as business owners.

Methodology

The methodology used for completing the primary market research was online survey research, consisting of eight questions asking small business owners a range of questions about their demographic information, their experiences starting their own companies, and their on-going needs while continuing to operate in the Middle Tennessee area.

Survey Results

The following gives a summary of the respondents surveyed:

Age range

The age range most commonly cited (40%) for small business owners was 45-54 years of age. The second most popular ranges were the 25-34 and 55-64 segments (both at 20%), followed by the 35-44 and 65-74 populations, both tied equally for third place (at 10%).

Annual Household Income

The Annual Household Income of most respondents (45%) was $35,000 – $49,999, followed by households containing $100,000 or more in second place (18%), households with $75,000 – $99,999 in third (at 15%), and households with $50,000 – $75,000 and less than $20,000 rounding out the final category (both at 10%). 2% of respondents chose not to answer this question.

Annual Sales

Annual Sales Revenues were most popular (40%) in the $100,000 – $249,999 range, followed by $20,000 – $49,999 as the second most popular range (25%), more than $250,000 and less than $5000 were listed as third (both at 10%), and Annual Sales of $5,000 – $19,999 was the fourth and final range (15%).

Software Programs Needed on Startup

Business owners identified the following software program needs when they first started their companies:

- Accounting/Bookkeeping/Financial Basics (45%)
- Marketing (20%)
- Website/Graphic Design Development (20%)
- E-Commerce (buying and selling online) (15%)

The most commonly cited software programs that small business owners said they needed most at their startup were: *1) Accounting/Bookkeeping/Financial Basics, 2) Marketing, and 3) Website/Graphic Design Development.*

Current Software Program Needs

Business owners surveyed identified the following as software programs they are currently in need of:

- Accounting/Bookkeeping/Financial Basics (65%)
- Website/Graphic Design Development (15%)
- E-Commerce (buying and selling online) (10%)
- Marketing (10%)

The most popular services cited were: *1) Accounting/Bookkeeping/Financial Basics, and 2) Website/Graphic Design Development.*

Where to look for Assistance?

When asked where they look for assistance in purchasing software for their small business, the entrepreneurs surveyed stated the following:

- Referrals from other business owners in same industry, friends, family, peers/networking groups via social networks (40%)
- The Internet/Google Searches (30%)
- Investors/Board Members/SCORE Counselors (13%)
- Information from Industry Associations relevant to their profession (9%)
- Books/Newspapers (8%)

Willingness to pay for Software Programs

Survey respondents were asked how much they'd be willing to pay for any of the software programs listed above. Most respondents (80%) said they'd be willing to pay $25 or 50, or between $51 – 100 per program for software they felt they needed in their business. The second most popular responses were between $101 – 150 per program or $151 or more (both at 10%).

Primary Market Profile

Based on the findings from the preliminary market research, 123 Accounting Plus Software has compiled the following market profile for the "ideal customer" for its software program:

- Targeted Age ranges: 25 – 34, 45 – 54, and 55 – 64.
- Targeted Annual Income ranges: $35,000 – $49,999 and $75,000 – $99,999.
- Annual Sales Revenue ranges: $50,000 or less and $100,000 – 249,999.
- Targeted Software Program: Accounting/Bookkeeping/Financial Basics.
- Targeted Price for Software Program: $75 per software suite, $25 for software upgrades.
- Targeted Marketing Medium: Using social media and peer group networking to build a clientele of digital "word-of-mouth" referral business.

Competitive Analysis

Currently, competitors for 123 Accounting Plus Software are free or low-cost open-source Accounting software platforms provided by companies offering additional software packages that address marketing and web design needs, or unverified entities who produce software programs without any additional support. Additionally, competition can be found from local Accounting and financial consulting firms in the Nashville and Middle Tennessee area that specialize in a variety of fields, yet offer services in Accounting as part of their overall catalog of many services.

The competitive advantage that 123 Accounting Plus Software offers over both the free and low cost fee-based alternatives offered by other companies, is that this company offers a dedicated Accounting software program with end-user support, specifically crafted for the purposes of serving small business Accounting needs. 123 Accounting Plus Software also improves the means by which clients connect to their customers, and enhances the overall company presence online and via traditional mediums through the long-term strengthening their brand.

As far as competing with local Accounting and financial services firms in the Middle Tennessee area, 123 Accounting Plus Software differentiates its service by focusing specifically in Accounting through our unique "My Accounting Plus" customization which provides company-specific small business Accounting profile and 24-hour customer support.

The Marketing Strategy

The following outlines the marketing strategy that 123 Accounting Plus Software intends to use to achieve the goals set forth in this marketing plan.

General Description

123 Accounting Plus Software is a software program specifically designed for small businesses accounting needs. It allows for unique customization for each licensee. The primary focus of the company is to provide Accounting software to small businesses without in-house Accounting departments. The marketing strategies used to capture clients that will utilize this service are: social media and peer networking, which will create referral business, in addition to online marketing through an online web presence via the company's website and social media outlets.

This activity requires the use of "guerilla marketing", a concept that works by investing time, ingenuity, and energy, over large monetary investments. Using the approach of "guerilla marketing", 123 Accounting Plus Software plans to build relationships with customers, based on their needs, and provide the products that address those needs to the customer's satisfaction.

Method of Sales and Distribution

Products offered by 123 Accounting Plus Software will be available online via direct sales from the company website.

Packaging

The 123 Accounting Plus Software package can be downloaded from the company website, and upon request, one hard copy a CD/DVD-Rom disc can also be shipped.

Pricing

The price for 123 Accounting Plus Software will be $75 per software license, and $25 for software upgrades.

Branding

Since 123 Accounting Plus Software is currently a name brand without recognition, the goal of the marketing strategy is to build the company and brand name over time by amassing a database of new customers and returning customers.

Online Branding

Search Engine Optimization (SEO)/Search Engine Marketing (SEM) campaigns will be used to maximize the amount of visitors to the 123 Accounting Plus Software company's website over time. Utilizing user-friendly and search engine-friendly web designs, the aforementioned site will use a combination of search engine-optimized text and Pay-Per-Click (PPC) advertising campaigns targeting keywords that can drive both organic search results as well as paid traffic to the site.

Promotion and Sales Strategy

The promotion and sales strategy employed will combine a mix of online and offline marketing tools. The 123 Accounting Plus Software company's website will be utilized for advertising product features, as well as for direct sales of the software program to the larger Internet public.

In an effort to build a clientele from a relatively unknown brand and unproven entity a "My Accounting Plus Special" will offer a reduced price for the first 100 purchasers of 123 Accounting Plus Software in exchange for customer testimonials.

Email Marketing

As a database of customer emerges, 123 Accounting Plus Software plans to effectively use an email marketing campaign to reach out for repeat business, both for the company's products and services. The company will offer customers the option of "opt-in/opt-out" in order to set their preferences on whether or not they want to be contacted about future related products or services.

The 123 Accounting Plus Software website will capture email addresses and produce a Newsletter on relevant survey research topics that will be disseminated at regular intervals, where each of the newsletter communications will be used to highlight the benefits of using the 123 Accounting Plus Software.
Reciprocal Marketing/Strategic Alliances

123 Accounting Plus Software plans to utilize the function of reciprocal marketing with companies that offer complimentary (though not directly competitive) services, as a means of strengthening the referral-based component of the company's marketing strategy.

Networking

Networking is a key component of 123 Accounting Plus Software marketing strategy, especially since a portion of the offline sales of the business is based on in-person networking/referral business. To that end, our company President will strategically join various professional/industry associations in the Middle Tennessee area, in an effort to network with as many business professionals and entrepreneurs as possible. Additionally, the President will attend workshops offered by Small Business Development Centers and other organizations focused primary on Small Business owners and aspiring entrepreneurs, and use those events as opportunities for making personal connections and publicizing the 123 Accounting Plus Software.

Specifically, on a monthly basis, the President will attend at least ten (10) regularly scheduled networking events throughout the Middle Tennessee area, including events held by the Nashville Area Chamber of Commerce, Brentwood Cool Springs Chamber of Commerce, Williamson County-Franklin Chamber of Commerce, Rutherford County Chamber of Commerce, Gallatin Area Chamber of Commerce, and Middle Tennessee rotary clubs, as well as group-specific networking opportunities available for women, entrepreneurs, and Accounting professionals.

Social Media Marketing

123 Accounting Plus Software will utilize social media outlets to drive traffic to its company website, generate interest in the software program, and generate sales to new customers and software upgrades to existing ones. In order to accomplish the social media marketing goals of this strategy, the company will do the following:

- Create a Twitter Accounting and send out daily messages about local businesses and small business Accounting tips.
- Create a Facebook Fan page (tied to Twitter updates) that allow for customers (i.e. Fans) to connect with the brand.
- Create a LinkedIn Accounting and send out daily messages about local businesses and small business Accounting tips
- Create a weekly contest to increase number of Facebook Fans.
- Create a weekly automated blog post to appear on the Facebook Fan page, Twitter, and LinkedIn Accountings.
- Give away a free "Small Business Accounting Tips" guide in exchange for emails that are captured through the company website.
- Use email addresses captured to send initial email sales offers, and period sales offers and Accounting tips.
- Partner with other Nashville and Middle Tennessee-based businesses on social media networks to generate leads and promote local events through Facebook, Twitter, LinkedIn, Public Calendars, and Meetup Groups.

Social Media Marketing Analytics

In order to measure the effectiveness of the social media marketing campaign set forth, the following analytics will be monitored:

- Number of web hits to the company website.
- Number of emails collected on the company website.
- Number of Facebook Fans.
- Number of Twitter Followers.
- Number of LinkedIn Connections.
- Number of people that attend special events advertised through our social media networks.
- Number of referrals from social media friends/followers/connections.
- Number of software licenses sold.
- Number of software upgrades sold to existing customers.

Assessment of Marketing Effectiveness

Monitoring the effectiveness of the company's marketing strategy is key for identifying new customer markets, gaining additional customer feedback, as well as assessing what marketing avenues work best. To accomplish this goal, the company will utilize a collection of online market surveys and customer questionnaires, and periodically analyze the information received for emerging trends and industry shifts. As an incentive for customers and visitors to the website, periodic random offers of remuneration (e.g. gift cards, free downloads, online prizes, etc.) will be extended in exchange for the customer completing a survey. The funding for these incentives is included in the monthly marketing budget.

Customer Service

Customer Service is an integral part of the marketing strategy for the company, as meeting customer's expectation for high quality products will help in establishing a dedicated customer base and achieving excellence. Every effort will be made by the company to insure that any issues related to customer satisfaction are promptly addressed, and that customer's expectations are met.

The Marketing and Sales Process

Now that you have gotten closer to validating your business idea, it's time to start thinking about how you will develop a marketing and sales process for your new venture. There is a six-step process to building customer evangelism — when your customer loves doing business with you so much that they sell for you.

Step 1. Build Awareness – Your target market is completely unaware of your product and service or company. Discuss how you will tell the world you are open for business.

Step 2. Create Comprehension – Your target market may have heard of your company, but are unaware of what you do. Discuss the benefits of your product or service.

Step 3. Create Conviction – Your target market understands your products and services, but they have no incentive to buy. Give them a reason to do business with you by doing your research so that you are positioned to solve their problem and make a sale.

Step 4. Create the Order – Your target market believes in your service, but they have not yet placed an order with you. Develop a process to monitor this warm lead so you can jump on any potential opportunities.

Step 5. Get the Reorder – Your best growth opportunity as a small business is to sell more to your existing customers. The key to being a sustainable business is reorders and up-sale opportunities. Develop a plan to keep your customers coming back.

Step 6. Generate Referrals – Many times, people will be receptive to new ideas when they are referred by someone they already know and trust. You need your customers to tell others about your products and services. How will you engage your loyal customers to pass along information to anyone interested in your products or service?

Your Turn: Brainstorm ideas for each step in the process. Choose one idea to implement and create a custom action plan for promoting your product or service.

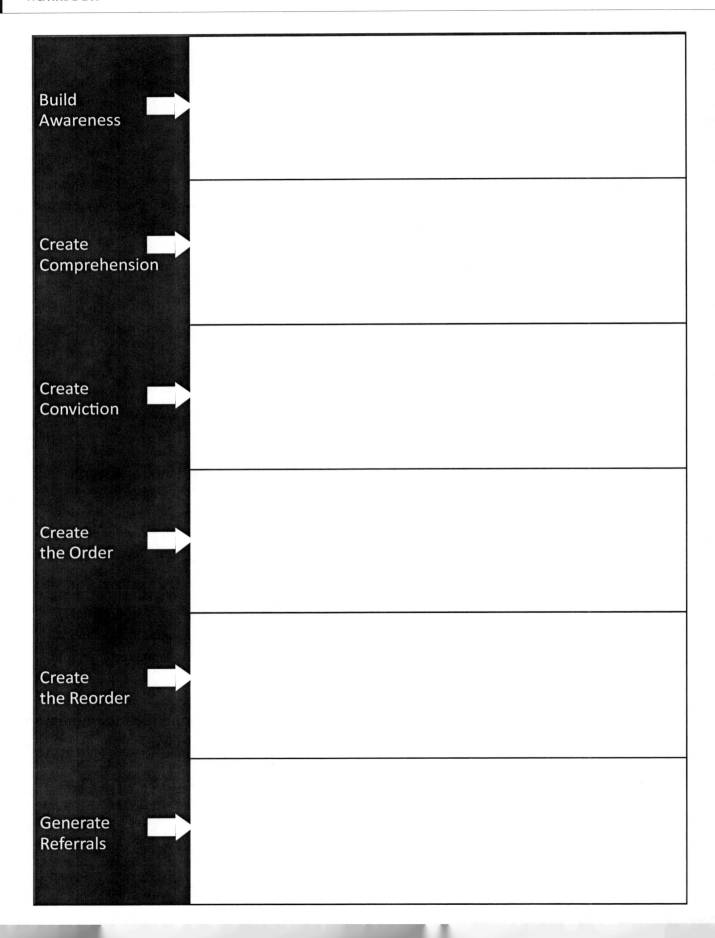

RECAP

- Your marketing plan is the life's blood of your business; that's why you need to develop it first.
- Identify who is buying and why.
- Validate that there's a real market for your product or service.
- Make sure you can see the face of your customer.
- Know the difference between marketing and advertising.
- Marketing is anything you do to get sales.
- Advertising is a specific tactic of marketing.
- Make it easy for the customer to make the purchase.

**Remember,
if you are not making money,
you have an expensive hobby.**

GETTING YOUR PRODUCT TO MARKET

Do you need money, manpower, manufacturing and marketing to get your product to market? What technical expertise do you need to deliver the product and what distribution channel will you use to deliver your goods to the customer? Good businesses die every day to due to undercapitalization or challenges with production or delivery. Make sure you consider what it will really take to make your business dream a reality. Outline the resources you need to have in place to deliver your product and the associated costs you expect. Match those costs up with your expected financing to determine if you have enough money to get off the ground. The logistics of your delivery should be clearly understood.

How will you get it to market?

Supply Channel	Sales Channel	Delivery Channel	Customer Receipt Timing
Local Vendors	Retail Store	Salesperson/Cashier	Now/Later
Manufacturer	Sales Representative	Warehouse	Later
Technical services workforce	Retail, Internet Service/ Call Centers, local media	Technician, service provider,	Now/later

Looking at the above examples, if you get your products from local venders (groceries, for instance) and you sell them through your retail store, your salesperson/cashier completes the transaction and your goods are sold. The customer takes receipt immediately. If you are selling furniture, however, the customer might not take delivery for several weeks. Having an idea of what your sales process is, no matter how simple it seems, can do nothing but help you be successful.

How will you meet the market's demand?

If your prime selling season is Christmas, your success will hinge on how fast you can "cash in" on the opportunity before the season ends. What sort of lead times do you need to gear up to meet the demand? It may take several months to get new inventory, which may be too late. Finally, there will be many up-front cash obligations to respond to this kind of seasonal business demand, so cash flow management is critical. If applicable, create a timeline starting with an anticipated sales period and work back to when the product must be in inventory (available for sale), when it must be paid for, to when it must be ordered from your manufacturer.

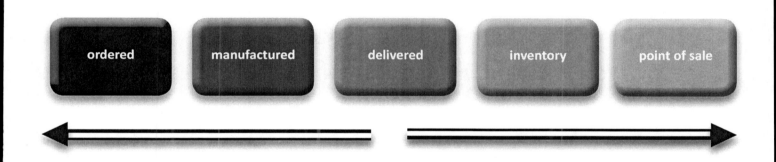

Two other questions about getting your product to market:

- How will you launch it?
- When will you launch it?

How will you ensure your idea has staying power?

You don't want to be too late to the market. Capitalizing on a fad is tricky business. Trends change quickly. It's like stock tips. By the time you hear the information, everybody has it and it might not be such a good buy any more. What you need to understand about a trend-driven business is that you want to make sure the product has enough staying power for you to make your money and cash out before the market moves again. Pet rocks, CB radios, raccoon hats, and mood rings, are items that were red hot, and now have lost their luster.

How will your business be relevant in the next 5 - 10 years?

Based on what you have developed, you now have all the information you need to decide whether or not you should move forward with the planning process to start your business.

BELOW, YOU WILL FIND A CHECKLIST THAT WILL ENABLE YOU TO MAKE YOUR FINAL "GO/NO GO DECISION".

	Yes	No	Working on it
Are you personally ready to become an entrepreneur?			
▪ Do you know what you want out of life as an entrepreneur?			
▪ Do you have the motivation required to be an entrepreneur?			
▪ Do you have the personality to be an entrepreneur?			
▪ Do you have the support systems in place?			
▪ Do you have the skills?			
▪ Do you have the time to invest in making your business a success?			
▪ Are you willing to change your lifestyle to become an entrepreneur?			
Are you financially ready to become an entrepreneur?			
▪ Can you financially afford to become an entrepreneur?			
▪ Are you willing to reduce your lifestyle down to just basic living expenses?			
▪ Are you financially prepared for your first year of business?			
▪ Do you have a plan to reduce/eliminate debt?			
▪ Is your credit in good shape?			
▪ Do you know your net worth?			
▪ Do you have a plan for health and life insurance?			
▪ Are you successfully managing your household budget?			

	Yes	No	Working on it

Have you starting thinking like an entrepreneur?

- Do you have outside advisers?
- Do you have an entrepreneurial mindset?
- Have you set healthy boundaries with family and friends?
- Do you have systems in place to stay motivated?
- Have you developed critical milestones based on your SMART goals?
- Are you reading what entrepreneurs read?

Is your business concept ready?

- Do you have a clear vision for your business?
- Do you have a business concept?
- Have you identified a need for your product or service?
- Can you easily explain the benefits of your product or service?
- Have you chosen a great name for your business?
- Can you easily explain the benefits of your product or service?
- Have you chosen a great name for your business?
- Have you identified your niche?
- Have you identified your ideal client?

Do you have a marketing plan?

- Do you have a marketing budget?
- Do you have a competitive price point?
- Do you have a signature move?
- Do you know who your competition is?
- Do you know the features and benefits of your product or service?

Do you have a Plan for Getting Your Product/Service to Market?

- Do you have the money to launch this business?
- Do have you have a sales channel?
- Do you have a supply channel?
- Do you know how you will meet the market demand?
- Does you idea has staying power?

NEXT STEPS:

Tally up all your Yeses! Think long and hard about your Nos. Now create an action plan with due dates for how you will turn you all your Nos into Yeses.

ACTION PLAN

1	Is your credit in good shape? No	Work with credit counselor to fix credit	Deadline: December 31
2			
3			
4			
5			
6			
7			
8			
9			
10			

RESOURCE GUIDE

Small business owners should set aside time each day to read about the business world. It's a mistake not to take advantage of the tremendous amount of information in books, web sites, blogs, magazines and newspapers. This reference section is packed with resources such as books, federal agencies, business associations, web resources, magazines, newspapers and blogs to get you started on your journey to learn all about the business of running a business. Enjoy!

BOOK REFERENCES

Ten Books Every Small Business Owner Should Read

How to Win Friends and Influence People by Dale Carnegie
First published in 1936, this is one of the best self-help books ever published with 15 million copies in print. This book touches on the fundamental techniques of handling people, six ways the make people like you, and 12 ways to win people to your way of thinking. Remember, people do business with people they like and people they know.

The 25 Most Common Sales Mistakes and How to Avoid Them by Stephen Schiffman
Schiffman is the man. This is one of my favorite small business books. This book is not only entertaining, but it also gets down to the fundamentals of being a killer salesperson, which should be every entrepreneur's goal. This book is practical, concise, and straight to the point.

Small Business Cash Flow by Denise O'Berry
Without cash flow, you don't have a business. Cash is king and Denise O'Berry gives straightforward advice on how to make your business a financial success. This book clearly provides strategies about how to manage and control your cash and also does a good job of pointing out how a small business owner can stay on top of cash flow issues. Remember, if your business in not making money, you may have just an expensive hobby.

Finance for Non-Finance Managers and Small Business Owners by Lawrence W. Tuller
This book takes the fear out of small business finance. It breaks down essential finance concepts including cash management, analyzing financial statements, forecasting, banks and bank terminology, operating budgets, and financing options.

Entrepreneurial Finance: Finance and Business Strategies for the Serious Entrepreneur by Steven Rogers
Professor Steven Rogers was distinguished by Fortune magazine as one of the Top 10 Minds in Small Business. Entrepreneurial Finance provides a straightforward, practical overview of the business and financial knowledge required to become a successful entrepreneur. This book also alerts entrepreneurs about the kind of financial problems they may face and recommends actions to prevent them.

The Wealthy Freelancer: 12 Secrets to a Great Income and an Enviable Lifestyle by Pete Savage, Steve Slaunwhite and Ed Gandia

Many people start out in business as freelancers or 1099 employees, so I thought it was important to highlight this terrific book on building a freelancing business. These three authors are pros at what they do. You need to have been in business at least five years or so to glean the knowledge you'll find in this book. You'll learn everything from the "practical tactical" such as how to prospect for clients, to the more "woo woo"(What do you mean?) things such as why keeping a positive mental attitude is so important. I highly recommend this book to small business owners who are just starting a freelance business or who have been in business a while and need to make more money.

The New Rules of Marketing and PR: How to Use Social Media, Blogs, News Releases, Online Video, and Viral Marketing to Reach Buyers Directly by David Meerman Scott

In 2007, when it was originally published, a friend suggested I read The New Rules of Marketing and PR and it changed my business. Now that David Meerman Scott has updated the book, it's an even better resource for integrating new school and old school marketing techniques with social media. By embracing the strategies in this book, you will transform your small business. Scott shows you a multitude of ways to propel yourself into becoming "THE" thought leader in your market and driving sales revenues – all without a huge budget.

The Seven Minute Difference by Allyson Lewis

What kind of small business coach would I be without a productivity book on the list? This book gives some really good advice on ways of improving your business habits as well as your personal life. This book especially gives you procrastinators out there things you can do now to be more effective.

Guerrilla Publicity by Jay Conrad Levinson, Rick Frishman, and Jill Lublin

Publicity as a marketing tool is probably one of the hardest things for a small business owner to master. Guerrilla Publicity makes it plain, and the suggestions are easy to implement. Even if you do not fashion yourself a PR machine, this book will help you learn this important skill needed for a successful business. This book will help you master the art of using free publicity as a key marketing tool. No small business can avoid this tool on the path to success.

The E-Myth Revisited by Michael E. Gerber

In The E-Myth Revisited, Michael E. Gerber explains a different approach to developing small businesses not just to survive, but with a plan to thrive. One of the best things about this book is Gerber's message around using the franchise model. He is not saying to buy a franchise. Instead, he wants us to develop processes and systems in our businesses so that we are not personally driving all the business revenue. I found the ideas in this book incredibly useful for my own business. He taught me how to systematize my business so that it could run without me. If you're a small business owner whose business is stagnant or going in the wrong direction, this book can be enormously valuable.

If you are one of these people who buy business books and never get around to reading them, consider subscribing to a service by Soundview Executive Book Summaries, www.summary.com. This company provides concise summaries of recently published business books.

If you have time to listen, but not to read, think about purchasing audio books. Each audio book can be downloaded to your iPod or MP3 player. If you have a long drive time, this is the perfect way to keep up with the latest small business trends and techniques.

Federal Resources

Census Bureau
The Census Bureau serves as the leading source of quality data about the nation's people and economy.
www.census.gov

Copyrights

U.S. Copyright Office
101 Independence Avenue SE
Washington, DC 20559-6000
(202) 707-3000
www.copyright.gov

Department of Labor

The Department of Labor promotes the welfare of the job seekers, wage earners, and retirees of the United States. They also track changes in employment, prices, and other national economic measurements.
www.dol.gov

Export.gov

A federal resource for information about markets and industries throughout the world.
www.export.gov

Federal Business Opportunities

The federal government's one stop virtual marketplace for all federal contracts.
www.FedBizOpps.gov

IRS

The IRS has a Small Business and Self-Employed Tax Center
www.irs.gov/businesses/small/

Minority Business Development Agency (MBDA)

This agency is part of the U.S. Department of Commerce and is the only federal agency created specifically to foster the establishment and growth of minority-owned businesses in America.
Call for locations at: 1-888-324-1551
www.mbda.gov

National Ombudsman (SBA program)

The National Ombudsman's primary mission is to assist small businesses when they experience excessive or unfair federal regulatory enforcement actions, such as repetitive audits or investigations, excessive fines, penalties, threats, retaliation or other unfair enforcement action by a federal agency.
www.sba.gov/aboutsba/sbaprograms/ombudsman/index.html

Occupational Safety and Health Administration (OSHA)

The Federal Occupational Safety and Health Administration (OSHA) outlines specific health and safety standards employers must provide for the protection of employees. Many states have similar standards.
http://www.osha.gov/dcsp/smallbusiness/index.html

Small Business Administration (SBA)

The Small Business Administration has many online resources, and the small business planner is really terrific. It provides information and resources that will help you at any stage of the business lifecycle.
http://www.sba.gov/smallbusinessplanner/index.html

SBA Training

The SBA also operates a web site that provides online training on many relevant issues for starting and growing a small business.
http://www.sba.gov/training/courses.html

Small Business Development Centers (SBDC)

SBDCs offer one-stop business assistance to current and prospective small businesses. Services include educational programs, advisory services, publications, financial programs and contract assistance. There are more than 1,100 SBDC centers across the country. For locations, call 1-800-8-ASK-SBA or use this link:
http://www.sba.gov/aboutsba/sbaprograms/sbdc/sbdclocator/SBDC_LOCATOR.html

SBDCNet

The Small Business Development Center National Information Clearinghouse serves as a resource providing timely, relevant research, Web-based information, and training to SBDC counselors and their small business clients.
www.sbdcnet.org

SCORE

Service Corps of Retired Executives known as the "Counselors to America's Small Business" or SCORE members, are successful retired business men and women who volunteer their time to assist aspiring small business owners.
www.score.org

Trademark Assistance Center

1-800-786-9199

TrademarkAssistanceCenter@uspto.gov

www.uspto.gov

Womenbiz.gov

This site is the gateway for women-owned businesses selling to the Federal Government.

www.womenbiz.gov

WEB RESOURCES

AllBusiness.com

This site has tons of small business information and sample forms and agreements. They have expert podcasts and videos on business topics, as well.

www.allbusiness.com

Alltop.com

Alltop organizes the site by topic. The small business "topic" has more than 100 different sites, including small business-related news and stories, and opinions and blogs.

www.alltop.com

Austin Family Business Program

Information and advice for running and working in a family business.

www.familybusinessonline.org

Bizstats.com

Instant access to useful financial ratios, business statistics and benchmarks, and effective and understandable online analysis of businesses and industries.

www.bizstats.com

Bplans.com

This web site contains the largest single collection of free sample business plans online. The site also includes interactive tools and a panel of experts who have answered more than 1,400 questions from people like you.

www.bplans.com

Business Owner's Tool Kit™

Business Owner's Toolkit™ offers more than 5,000 pages of free cost-cutting tips, step-by-step checklists, real-life case studies, startup advice, and business templates to small business owners and entrepreneurs.

www.toolkit.com

Fedmarket.com
This non-profit organization is all about information on how to sell to the federal government. They have over 100 pages of valuable procurement-related articles, information, and links and offer live seminars and trade shows on marketing your services to the government.
www.fedmarket.com

Franchise Registry
The registry helps lenders speed access to SBA financial assistance during the loan review process for franchisees. The Registry enables lenders and SBA local offices to verify a franchise system's lending eligibility through the Internet.
www.franchiseregistry.com

FranNet
Franchise experts help you learn about the many choices available and how to select the right opportunity for you.
www.frannet.com

Hoover's, Inc.
This service delivers comprehensive company, industry, and market intelligence on more than 14 million companies, with in-depth coverage of 42,000 of the world's top businesses. Reports are generated for a fee.
www.hoovers.com

IBISWorld
IBISWorld is a leader in gathering business data to help you do industry analysis for your business plan. This is a fee-based service.
www.ibisworld.com

Loopnet.com
The largest online database of commercial real estate for sale and for lease. Search for Land, Office, Retail, Industrial, Apartments, Hotels and other types of property.
www.loopnet.com

Microsoft Small Business Center
Microsoft provides advice, products, technology tools and information for your small businesses.
microsoft.com/smallbusiness/hub.mspx

MoreBusiness.com
This free web site provides a wealth of useful articles, sample business plans, business tips, insight, a free Intranet and other materials to help small businesses grow.
www.morebusiness.com

My Own Business, Inc.
A non-profit organization committed to helping you succeed. Their team of business experts have unselfishly contributed their experience and knowledge to help you succeed in business.
http://www.myownbusiness.org/

NOLO
The nation's leading provider of do-it-yourself legal solutions for small businesses. Its goal is to help people handle their own everyday legal matters — or learn enough about them to make working with a lawyer a more satisfying experience.
www.nolo.com/category/sb_home.html

Public Entity Risk Institute (PERI)
PERI produces a web site with relevant and high quality risk management information, training, data, and data analysis. The web site also features an extensive resource library organized by topic, audience, and type of resource.
www.riskinstitute.org/peri

Zoomerang
An online survey software that businesses, organizations and individuals use to create professional, customized surveys.
www.zoomerang.com

BUSINESS ASSOCIATIONS

American Management Association (AMA)
A world leader in professional development, advancing the skills of individuals to drive business success. AMA supports the goals of individuals and organizations through a complete range of products and services, including seminars, webcasts and podcasts, conferences, corporate and government solutions, business books and research.
http://www.american-management-association.org

American Society of Association Executives (ASAE)
The best resource to locate a trade organization in your industry.
www.asaenet.org

Angel Forum, LLC
Private equity group which provides technology and non-technology pre-screened companies seeking equity financing of $100,000 to $1 million, delivers "live" presentations to pre-screened private and corporate investors.
www.angelsforum.com

Association of Women's Business Centers
Women Business Development Centers (WBDC) provide direct educational services to women business owners. Many centers also certify women business enterprises (WBEs).
www.awbc.biz

Better Business Bureau (BBB)
Check out a business; find a local Better Business Bureau, and more.
www.us.bbb.org

Insurance Information Institute (III)
The Insurance Information Institute (www.iii.org) has great resources for small business owners. They have a small business owner's guide to insurance section that is worth looking at. Log on at
http://www.iii.org/individuals/business/small_business.html

International Franchise Association (IFA)
The International Franchise Association, founded in 1960, is a membership organization of franchisors, franchisees, and suppliers.
www.franchise.org

Marathon Club
The Marathon Club is focused on increasing the availability and investment of private equity capital into enterprises that have significant minority ownership and management participation.
www.marathonclub.org

National Association of Manufacturers (NAM)
The NAM's mission is to advocate on behalf of its members to enhance the competitiveness of manufacturers. NAM is a primary source for information on manufacturers' contributions to innovation and productivity.
www.nam.org

National Association of the Self Employed (NASE)
NASE was founded in 1981 and represents hundreds of thousands of entrepreneurs and micro-businesses, and is the largest nonprofit, nonpartisan association.
www.nase.org

National Association of Small Business Investment Companies
Small business investment companies (SBIC) and Specialized Small Business Investment Companies (SSBIC) invest in small businesses. These are private venture capital firms licensed by the SBA.
www.nasbic.org

National Association of Women Business Owners (NAWBO)
The largest women's business organization in the U.S., with 80 chapters across the country.
www.nawbo.org

National Business Incubation Association (NBIA)
NBIA is a private, nonprofit 501(c)(3) membership organization considered the world's leading organization advancing business incubation and entrepreneurship. It's mission is to provide training and a clearinghouse for information on incubator management and development issues and on tools for assisting start-up and fledgling firms.
www.nbia.org

National Federation of Independent Business (NFIB)
A national small business association in Washington, D.C., and all 50 state capitals. NFIB gives small and independent business owners a voice in shaping the public policy issues that affect their business.
www.nfib.com

National Foundation for Teaching Entrepreneurship (NFTE)
The National Foundation for Teaching Entrepreneurship helps young people from low-income communities build skills and unlock their entrepreneurial creativity.
www.nfte.com

National Minority Supplier Development Council (NMSDC)
The National Minority Supplier Development Council provides a direct link between corporate America and minority-owned businesses. NMSDC is a purchasing council for nationally certified minority business enterprises or (MBEs).
www.nmsdc.org

National Restaurant Association
The National Restaurant Association is the leading business association for the restaurant industry.
www.restaurant.org

National Urban League (NUL)
The nation's oldest and largest community-based movement devoted to empowering African Americans to enter the economic mainstream. Many of the NUL's 100 affiliates operate Economic Empowerment Centers. EEC Centers bring together top private, public and nonprofit organizations to improve minority entrepreneurship in economically underserved urban areas nationwide.
www.nul.org

Private Equity
Active Capital (originally known as ACE-Net) provides information to angel investors on small, dynamic, growing businesses seeking private equity financing.
www.activecapital.org

Risk Management Association

This association produces the most reliable information on the study of financial performance and ratios of over 600 industries. They sell their annual studies online for a nominal fee.

www.rmahq.org/online_prods/onlineprods.html

Small Business Legislative Council (SBLC)

The Small Business Legislative Council (SBLC) is an independent, permanent coalition of trade and professional associations who share a common concern for the future of small business.

http://www.sblc.org

Social Venture Network (SVN)

A non-profit network who's mission is to inspire a community of business leaders to build socially and environmentally sustainable business in the 21st century. SVN champions this effort through initiatives, information services and twice annual conferences.

www.svn.org

Society for Human Resource Management

Leading organization of HR directors and staff. This web site is packed with insightful articles on numerous human resource topics.

www.shrm.com

U.S. Chamber of Commerce

The world's largest business federation. The Chamber's core purpose is to fight for free enterprise before Congress, regulatory agencies, the courts, the media, and governments around the world.

www.uschamber.com

U.S. Hispanic Chamber of Commerce

In 1979, the Hispanic business community in the United States envisioned the need for a national organization to represent its interests before the public and private sectors. They are the umbrella organization for Hispanic chambers across the country.

www.ushcc.org

Venture Capital Institute

The organization conducts seminars for professional venture capitalists and entrepreneurs.

www.vcinstitute.org

Women's Business Enterprise National Council (WBENC)

WBENC is a purchasing council for nationally certified women's business enterprises known as WBEs.

www.wbenc.org

MAGAZINES AND NEWSPAPERS

Every business owner should subscribe to at least one industry trade publication and the local Business Journal (Is this a national chain?) newspapers to generate leads to stay connected with the regional business community.

American City Business Journals
Bizjournals is the new media division of American City Business Journals, the nation's largest publisher of metropolitan business newspapers. It operates the web sites for each of the company's 41 print business journals.
www.bizjournals.com

Black Enterprise (BE)
This monthly business magazine is so relevant, I can't bring myself to throw one away. I keep a personal library. BE is the preeminent African American destination for information regarding entrepreneurship, technology and personal finance. Their online resources and business conferences are excellent, as well.
www.blackenterprise.com

Entrepreneur Magazine
A solid publication with innovative solutions for small business owners. Their web site also features exhaustive resources, back issues and tools for entrepreneurs. I especially like their start-up and women entrepreneur sections online.
www.entrepreneur.com

Inc. Magazine
Inc. is the gold standard of small business news. This monthly publication provides timely information on industry trends, innovative small businesses, and offers ideas on how to improve your business. Inc.com provides additional information and advice covering virtually every business and management task. It also includes the Inc. magazine archives, more than 100 free tools to help you in every area of your business, and has regular columnists and blogs on the site.
www.inc.com/tools

Wall Street Journal
In addition to being the gold standard business publication, WSJ offers a small business web site featuring businesses for sale, franchises, and other business opportunities and many other articles and resources relevant to small business development. The also have a blog at Wall Street Journal Online titled Independent Street.
http://www.startupjournal.com/
blog: www.online.wsj.com/small-business

TOP 5 SMALL BUSINESS BLOGS THAT I THINK ALL SMALL BUSINESS OWNERS SHOULD READ.

Succeed As Your Own Boss Blog

www.succeedasyourownboss.com

This blog is written by Melinda Emerson, the "SmallBizLady," and the author of Become Your Own Boss in 12 Months and this workbook. The blog focuses on start-up success techniques, branding, how to grow, cash flow and finance, and social media marketing. The blog also features weekly interviews with business experts from the Twitter talk show #Smallbizchat.

SmallbizTrends

www.smallbiztrends.com

This blog is written and managed by Anita Campbell. She has her finger on the pulse of small businesses. Her blog provides news, insights and the latest trends and developments in small business. Smallbiztrends reaches over 1,000,000 entrepreneurs annually.

Small Biz Technology

www.smallbiztechnology.com

This blog is written by Ramon Ray, editor and technology evangelist of Smallbiztechnology.com. This web site is all about helping "regular" small business owners (those who are not technically savvy), know what technology they need to boost productivity, save time, increase revenue, and boost customer service for their business.

Duct Tape Marketing

www.ducttapemarketing.com/blog

This blog is written by John Jantsch, the Duct Tape Marketing guy. The blog has lots of great coaching, audio and video posts and other resources along with links to free marketing plans and other documents and business resources.

Copyblogger

www.copyblogger.com

This blog is written by Brian Clark. He writes one of the best blogs on how to write for the web and he's a great writer to boot. You can learn a lot about excellent content from this well-written blog.

CPSIA information can be obtained at www.ICGtesting.com
Printed in the USA
266329BV00003B/2/P

9 780979 983917